Career Survival

Strategic Job and Role Planning

Edgar H. Schein, Ph.D.
MIT Sloan School of Management

Pfeiffer
& COMPANY

Johannesburg • Oxford
San Diego • Sydney • Toronto

Editor: JoAnn Padgett
Assistant Editor: Heidi Erika Callinan
Interior Page Design: Susan G. Odelson
Cover Design: John Odam Associates

Library of Congress Cataloging-in-Publication Data
Schein, Edgar H.
   Career survival: strategic job and role planning/Edgar H. Schein.
     p.   cm.
   Includes bibliographical references and index.
   ISBN 0-89384-241-9 (pbk.: alk. paper)
   1. Career development.   I. Title.
HF5381.S347 1994
658.3'124–dc20
                          95-26533
                          CIP

Printing 1 2 3 4 5 6 7 8 9 10

Contents

CHAPTER 3
Step 1: Inventory Current Job and Roles 19

CHAPTER 4
Step 2: Identify Changes in the Environment 35

▼▼▼ Indicates exercise

▼▼▼ Indicates exercise

CHAPTER 9

Conclusions and Implications   89

Preface

Most managers and employees will agree that the rate of change in organizations is accelerating. One of the major changes is that jobs themselves are becoming less well-defined. If the predictions about less hierarchy and more horizontal, project-based work are accurate, most managerial, professional, and technical employees will find themselves switching roles frequently.

Job descriptions will become increasingly useless because 1) they are designed to create and maintain stability; and 2) they do not put enough emphasis on how jobs and roles relate to one another. In their place, we need a dynamic process that

— Allows job holders to redefine their changing roles and adapt to a turbulent environment

— Helps executives and managers track how roles in their organizations are changing and communicate those changes to future job holders

The strategic job and role planning described in this book is just such a dynamic process. The book's activities and conceptual materials are based on research that was first reported in *Career Dynamics: Matching Individual and Organizational Needs*. The methodology has been elaborated and tested frequently since then through workshops in a variety of organizations.

Who Needs to Do Job and Role Planning?

Everyone should regularly evaluate their job to identify if career goals are in sync with the marketplace and with long-range individual plans. However, the following groups of employees need to make job and role planning a priority.

— Technical, professional, and managerial employees and executives who are in organizations experiencing change
— Managers who are involved in succession planning and/or career counseling of subordinates
— Employees who are uncertain or confused about their job responsibilities or who are accepting new assignments

As an employee, job and role planning will help you

— Understand the social network in which your job is embedded
— Identify your job's requirements and its key "stakeholders"

— Increase your understanding of your organization and its dynamics
— Analyze the impact of your organization's change process

As a manager, job and role planning will help you

— Understand how your job impacts your subordinates and what their expectations of you might be
— Explain dynamic job elements to subordinates and how to prepare for their jobs in the future
— Relate your own and your subordinates' work to the organization's mission and strategy
— Do more effective organizational and human resource planning

Introduction

How Does Job and Role Planning Work?

The job and role planning activity leads you through a series of steps that helps you understand

— How your job relates to other people's expectations of you
— Key stakeholders of your job
— Key stakeholder's expectations of you
— Anticipated changes in the work environment
— The impact of the changes on the stakeholders and their expectations
— The implications of all these things for your job

What Do I Have to Do?

The process described in this book can be used in two ways: You can analyze your own job and roles by completing the steps on your own, or you can complete the steps with several others. The latter is preferable because the kind of information you need in order to achieve maximum insight is often easier to elicit in a group context.

The activity should take no more than two hours of your time, although it can take longer if you choose to dig deeper into some of the issues that will surface.

All you need is this book and something to write with. If you are working in a group, a flip chart and wall space on which to hang the flip chart pages are also desirable.

CHAPTER 1

Strategic Job and Role Planning

Why Is It So Important?

Strategic job and role planning is a new technique designed to overcome some of the weaknesses of traditional methods of job analysis, human resource planning, and job design. It recognizes that the nature of work is changing rapidly and that work is increasingly embedded in a complex set of relationships. One cannot adequately design or describe a job without explicitly considering those relationships—the "role network" that surrounds the job. In that role network, there always will be key stakeholders whose expectations define the essence of the job. The identification of those stakeholders, a description of their particular expectations, and a projection of how those expectations may change as one analyzes changes in the environment become crucial elements in both work design and human resource planning.

Most human resource planning processes bypass job and role planning and go directly to the questions: "What kinds of people do we need" and "how many will fulfill our plans?" The hidden and dangerous assumption in this approach is that the *work* to be done will remain more or less the same and one needs to look only at the potential and performance of the available people.

Yet in example after example of succession planning with which I have been involved, the key questions actually turned out to be

1. Will the job itself change over the next few years?

2. In what ways will the content of the job and the role network around the job change?

3. What new motives, skills, and attitudes will be required to do the new kind of work?

4. What do these changes mean in terms of the kind of person who should be hired or promoted into the job?

5. What do these changes mean in terms of the kind of training and development that need to be designed for job incumbents?

There is a need to answer these questions at both the organizational and the individual levels. The organization needs the information in order to do its human resource planning, and the individual needs the information in order to structure his or her own priorities. The individual part becomes more important as the boundaries of jobs and roles become more fluid and as organizations increasingly give people more autonomy in designing and structuring elements of their own jobs.

The activity and the reading materials in this book are focused both on the *content of the job itself* and on the *network of relationships* in which the job is embedded. Typically, both of these change as the organization's strategies and plans are revised to adapt to a fluid environment. That is why the activity is called "strategic job and role planning."

Every manager and employee should conduct an annual job and role analysis of his or her own job and should participate with others in analyzing the jobs of all subordinates, key peers, and superiors with whom organizational relationships exist. An organization cannot achieve its strategic objectives until they have been translated into concrete goals. Those goals cannot be met until they have been clearly understood by the job holders. Such understanding requires not only self-insight but also clear communication of expectations on the part of managers, peers, and subordinates. Joint job and role planning through the application of open-systems planning to specific jobs is the means of achieving such understanding and insight.

Applying Open-Systems Planning to Jobs and Roles

Most organizations recognize that some form of open-systems planning is necessary in order to understand strategic options and to formulate concrete plans. It is logical that the same kind of planning be done for all major jobs and roles in the organization, taking into account what new strategic directions may have been formulated by top management and what changes may have occurred in the context in which a given job operates.

Only through systematic job and role analysis and planning and by clear communication of the results can a manager meet the needs of the organization to fulfill its basic mission. In addition, the information generated by job and role planning is needed to help human resources

— Plan for staffing, succession, and employee and management development
— Determine the critical dimensions to be used in performance appraisal and the judgment of potential
— Inventory human resources
— Design appropriate reward and control systems

The essential elements of open-systems planning as applied to jobs and roles are to

1. Identify the role network and the major stakeholders surrounding a given job and roles in the organization

2. Analyze the current expectations, demands, and constraints of each stakeholder

3. Project what environmental changes will occur in the near future (one to five years)

4. Analyze the major impacts these environmental changes will have on each of the stakeholders and determine whether the role network itself will change

5. Analyze how these changes will affect stakeholder expectations, demands, and constraints pertaining to the job and roles

6. Determine what the implications are for job and role incumbents in terms of the qualifications and experience they should have to fulfill the job and roles

This kind of analysis is in sharp contrast to the typical job evaluation exercise that asks the individual to list job requirements and then asks for a self-analysis of skills, preferred activities, areas of enjoyment, and so on. Job and role planning puts each job into its appropriate organizational context and assumes the following:

— The major stakeholders surrounding a given job will change.
— The expectations of given stakeholders will change as the environment changes.

The most important thing to understand about a job or role, then, is how future expectations pertaining to it will change. Only when that is understood can you analyze how your own skills and preferences will fit with a given job. Too often, we take jobs that fit us today without realizing that, in the future, the job will make demands on us that we may not be able to meet.

Some Concrete Examples

The Changing Nature of Plant Management

The clearest example of the need for job and role analysis and planning that I have observed has been in the chemical industry, where the job of plant manager has, in some settings, undergone almost total transformation. I have done job and role planning with teams of plant managers both in the U.S. and in Europe. Typically, the assumption was that the job primarily was a technical one and that the dominant trend was the increasing technological complexity of the manufacturing process. Therefore, the task was perceived to be to ensure that the pool of future plant managers would be technically competent to handle the increasing complexity.

When the people involved were asked to identify all the stakeholders that have expectations of a plant manager and to analyze how their expectations may change in the future, a somewhat different picture emerged. First of all, the analysis revealed that the technical content of the typical plant manager's job had already become so heavy that the plant manager needed a technical staff. He or she could no longer stay on top of the technology, and key technical decisions were made primarily by the staff.

The stakeholder analysis revealed that there were powerful changes occurring in the attitudes of the unions, the community, and the relevant government agencies that had little to do with technological niceties of the production process, except where it specifically impacted safety, quality of work life, or the environment. In each relationship with a stakeholder, the plant manager was perceived to be doing more *negotiating* in a complex political environment. One company realized that it needed future plant managers who were talented negotiators and who were able to work on the plant's various *external interfaces.* Internal relations and technical matters increasingly were handled by the manager's staff and subordinates.

The job had been changing for a number of years, but this had not been explicitly observed or analyzed, hence, little provision had been made in the human resource planning and development processes to identify and develop such negotiators. Individual plant managers experienced sudden insight into the causes of their frustrations; they felt unprepared to do things outside their formal job descriptions. As a result, the company instituted a different system of appraising performance and potential in the manufacturing-management area and started new development programs to ensure that it could fulfill its vision of the job's future.

Plant managers who participated in the activity had a sense of relief that what they were experiencing was valid, not simply an indication that they were doing a bad job or concentrating on the wrong things. They were able to clarify in their own minds the importance of managing the external interfaces and, more importantly, now found it legitimate to ask for training and advice in these more "soft" and political skills.

Spontaneous Redesign of a Job or Role

The power of job and role analysis was illustrated by another company that lost its vice president for administration. I was working with the company in a one-day workshop on career development. During lunch, the president and his other key subordinates said that I could hang around but pardoned themselves to decide who should replace the lost executive.

It turned out that they had one candidate in mind, Joe, but they had some reservations about him. I listened for about a half hour while they discussed all the pros and cons of giving Joe the job, citing Joe's strengths and weaknesses in general personality terms and in terms of past job history. He was a good manager, but he was not so good in external relationships; he handled people well; he knew the technical areas of the company well, etc. In general, the picture was very positive, but somehow the group members could not agree that he was right for the job.

At this point, I became curious about the job itself and asked quite innocently what the vice president for administration did, who the major stakeholders surrounding the job were, and what the executives perceived that job to entail in the future. The group members started to list things such as personnel, legal, purchasing, information systems, and public relations. When they came to this last item, someone interrupted and said, "You know, as I think about it,

Joe is good in all of those areas except public relations. He is just not good with outsiders and, as we look ahead, those outsider relationship are going to become much more important."

This comment produced immediate agreement from all members and led one of them to the big insight. He asked the group whether public relations had to be part of the job. After only a few minutes thought, the group agreed that public relations did not have to be part of the job, that, in fact, the other parts were growing so rapidly that there already was enough in the job, and that they easily could shift public relations to one of the other senior vice presidents until a person could be found to do solely public relations. Once they had redesigned the job, they immediately reached agreement on Joe's appropriateness for it, and, incidentally, discovered that public relations was going to become so important in the future that they needed a full-time person to handle it.

This example illustrates the importance of doing job and role analysis and planning for key executive positions in a group that has the power to redesign the management system. We often assume that the present structure of jobs is appropriate and reexamine individual jobs only when major reorganizations occur. But restructuring of the sort that this group did will become more and more common as the environment becomes more dynamic and as stakeholder expectations change.

Discovering the Complexity of Human Resource Management

Many human resource managers complain that they are not clear about how to do their jobs—are they professional experts, counselors, servants of power who help top management to implement policies, helpers to line managers to handle their human problems for them, legal advisers to keep management from getting sued on affirmative-action violations, or what? Job and role analysis and planning with groups of HR managers typically has revealed that there are basically four sets of stakeholders and that the complexity of the job results from changing expectations on the part of those stakeholders.

Senior management as a set of stakeholders increasingly expects the human resource function to participate in strategic discussions by helping to forecast human resource requirements and issues and, at the same time, to administer all of the human resource systems such as compensation, benefits, performance appraisal, and training more and more efficiently.

Line managers as stakeholders expect their human resource managers to solve "people problems" for them and to be supportive helpers in running their operations. Some line managers expect the human resource manager to be an adviser; others expect him or her to actually do the hiring, firing, appraisal, counseling, training, career planning, and so on. Many line managers also expect the human resource manager to be a competent organization development professional who can facilitate meetings, design team-building programs, and in other ways help to make the organization more effective.

Projecting into the future reveals that the "servicing the line" function is declining as more line managers see their own responsibilities for human resource management increasing and, at the same time, the "organization development" function is increasing as line managers see the growing need for collaborative relationships, team building, and organizational learning.

A third stakeholder that is playing an increasingly important role is the professional community of human resource management, which expects the individual manager to run a "professional" operation and to be an expert in those functions that are clearly at the heart of human resource management, such as compensation, employee development, counseling, etc.

A fourth set of stakeholders is composed of the employees, who expect the human resource person to be a champion, ombudsperson, and protector of their rights and privileges. The whole grievance process in employee relations reflects the potentially conflicting expectations of top management, which wants to solve problems without strikes or other inconveniences, and the employees, who want protection and improvements in the quality of their working lives.

As groups of human resource managers examine how the expectations of these four groups impact them, they become clearer about the ambiguity of their jobs, the "role overload" they often feel, and the role conflicts that are inherent in the job. More importantly, as they analyze how the environment is impacting the stakeholders, they gain increasing insight into what will be demanded of them in the future. For example, as companies are becoming more global, top management is expecting more expertise in the management of overseas assignments, cultural diversity, and other issues that derive from working in multicultural environments. As the world is becoming more conscious of ethical and value issues, employees increasingly expect more autonomy and flexibility in their working situations. As the boundaries of line manager's jobs are becoming more fluid, and as hierarchy increasingly is being supplemented with other coordination mechanisms such as complex matrices and rotating project management, line managers will expect more help of an unspecified nature. It is also possible that anxiety levels in the organization will increase dramatically and that human resource managers will have to serve more as individual counselors.

Thus, strategic job and role planning reveals not only how jobs will change, but also why jobs feel as they do, why sometimes one feels overloaded or in conflict. The insights obtained through this activity help you to manage feelings and negotiate a situation that may be more compatible with your skills and preferences. (Chapter 3 of this book explores some ways to deal with such issues.)

Job and Role Planning Output As Job Description

This section focuses on using job and role analysis as a tool for understanding one's job. The importance of this was illustrated by a group of senior managers who were analyzing their own roles as part of a general strategy process. They carefully assessed the stakeholders, the environmental changes that would occur, the changing expectations of the stakeholders, the impacts that those changes would have on the job of senior manager, and the qualifications that were crucial in any future holder of the job. All of this was summarized on five flip-chart pages as output from the group discussion.

At the end of the two hours of work, one of the group members said, "You know, I wish that when I received my promotion into this job, someone had handed me something like those five pages. That would have been infinitely more helpful to me in figuring out what I was supposed to do than the dry, dated, and static job description. If I could have had the benefit of this kind of thinking, I would have become productive much faster." How many job holders do you think would say the same thing?

Conclusion

For any job in the organization, it is necessary once a year or so to review what is happening to that job and to project those changes into the future. Only when that is done explicitly do we have a basis for human resource planning and for determining explicitly what the organization needs to fulfill its strategic objectives. And only then do job holders have an accurate sense of what their own priorities must be as they look ahead to the future.

The rest of this book is devoted to helping you to do job and role analysis and planning. First it will review the basic steps that need to be followed, then it will provide some conceptual material to aid in the analysis that accompanies each step. It is suggested that you read these materials before you attempt to do the actual activity.

CHAPTER 2

Job and Role Analysis and Planning

The following summarizes the steps in the job and role analysis and planning process. It introduces you to the concepts and terms used in the subsequent chapters.

Step 1. Inventory Current Job and Roles

The analysis involves the identification of one's complete stakeholder/role network and the key dimensions of one's job. The role network includes all the people who have some expectations of the person whose job is being analyzed. The key stakeholders are those members of the role network whose own work will be affected severely if the job holder does not meet their expectations. This analysis can be done alone, but it is preferable to work with two or three colleagues, peers, subordinates, or supervisors who are part of the role network of the job. The process for carrying out the analysis is provided in Chapter 3.

Step 2. Identify Changes in the Environment

Every job and role and the associated stakeholders exist within an environment created partly by the organization and partly by outside forces. Environments can be analyzed from technological, economic, political, interpersonal, and sociocultural aspects. A systematic scan of each of these aspects will reveal some probable changes that will impact the stakeholders and their expectations. Changes in those expectations will, in turn, impact the job being analyzed. This analysis is described in Chapter 4.

Step 3. Assess Environmental Impacts on Stakeholder Expectations

Given the environmental changes that have been identified in step 2, what impacts will these have on the expectations of each set of stakeholders? This step asks you to analyze and rate each of these impacts on the job or role itself. Each impact is rated as crucial or peripheral. Those impacts identified as crucial are described in detail, using the tools presented in Chapter 5.

Step 4. Determine the Impact on Job and Roles

In this step, the identified impacts are summarized and analyzed from a more global perspective and the job or role is redefined accordingly. What will be most different about this job in the future? What dimensions will change and how? Chapter 6 describes the procedure to be used.

Step 5. Redefine Job Requirements

What are the implications of the analysis in Step 4 for the kinds of people who should be considered for this job? What kinds of skills, motives, and talents will be needed in future occupants of the job? If you are analyzing your own job, what are the implications for yourself? Will you need some new training or experience? Are you mismatched to the job? Should you attempt to restructure the job? Chapter 7 provides guidelines for doing this analysis.

Step 6. Extend the Strategic Job and Role Planning Activity

Because every job is part of a network, the basic analysis should reveal what other jobs are also changing, thereby identifying the next steps in the job and role planning process. Once some people have used the process successfully, they can teach others in group settings.

CHAPTER 3

Step 1:
Inventory Current Job
and Roles

▼▼▼ *Basic Job Dimensions*

Use your job description and anything else (such as performance-appraisal forms) to identify the primary dimensions of your job. Start by listing your basic responsibilities, your primary resources for getting the job done (subordinates, budgets, equipment) and, finally, the main skills, talents, and attitudes required to do your job.

▼ Basic Responsibilities

▼ Primary Resources for Getting the Job Done

▼ Skills, Talents, and Attitudes Required to Do the Job

▼▼▼ *Job and Role Profile*

If you have managerial or project responsibilities, you may want to evaluate your job on the following dimensions, which highlight areas of change. The ratings will provide you with a baseline against which to compare your job in the future.

Rate your behavior in your current job using the five-point scale: "1" is low; "5" is high.

		Low				High
1.	Work with and in groups of various sorts (committees, task forces, meetings, etc.)	1	2	3	4	5
2.	Operate as a consultant/catalyst in my day-to-day roles	1	2	3	4	5
3.	Integrate the efforts of others who are technically more competent in their specialties than I am	1	2	3	4	5
4.	Rely on secondhand information that is gathered by others	1	2	3	4	5
5.	Monitor the thinking and decision making of others rather than doing it myself	1	2	3	4	5

6. Facilitate the processes of manage-   1 2 3 4 5
   ment and decision making rather than
   making the decisions myself

7. Identify relevant problems and make   1 2 3 4 5
   sure that the right problems are worked
   on

8. Depend on others (peers, subordinates,   1 2 3 4 5
   etc.) for total performance (rather than
   it being within my own control)

9. Level of responsibility (accountability) is   1 2 3 4 5
   greater than my direct degree of control

10. Spend time considering the long-range   1 2 3 4 5
    health of the organization rather than
    its day-to-day performance

▼▼▼ Current Role Network and Key Stakeholders

This activity will help you identify your *role network* (the people who expect things of you) and your *key stakeholders* within that network (those whose own work or life would be upset if you did not meet their expectations).

Notice that although your job is the focus of this analysis, your role network probably will include family, friends, and community members who also expect some of your time, effort, and commitment. In terms of key stakeholders, some of these people may be more central than some of your coworkers. A sample role network is provided on the next page.

On the following page, draw your own role network. Put yourself in the center and then draw all the members of your role set around you, identifying them either by name or title. Draw arrows from each to you and from you to each of them. Make the thickness of each arrow represent how important the link is or how extensive the expectations of the stakeholder are.

Think broadly about all categories of stakeholders: your bosses, subordinates, peers, internal and external customers, internal and external suppliers, regulating bodies, colleagues outside your immediate job, your spouse or significant other, your children, special friends, and community members.

Do this thoroughly so you can appreciate the complexity of the network in which your job is embedded.

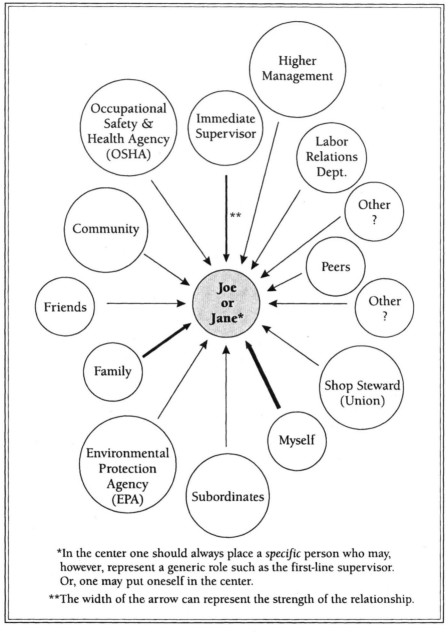

*In the center one should always place a *specific* person who may,
however, represent a generic role such as the first-line supervisor.
Or, one may put oneself in the center.

**The width of the arrow can represent the strength of the relationship.

Sample Role Network of a First-Line Supervisor

▼▼▼ *Role Network*

▼ Draw your own role network on this page.

▼▼▼ *Critical Stakeholders and Their Expectations*

Go back over your diagram and pick out five or six stakeholders whose expectations influence you the most. To help identify them, ask yourself who would be most upset if you failed to meet their expectations. Add yourself because you also have a job concept and self-expectations.

Write down the most important expectations of each of the critical stakeholders. If you are not sure what their expectations are, put down your best guess.

▼ Stakeholder 1:

▼ Major Expectations:

▼ Stakeholder 2:

▼ Major Expectations:

▼ Stakeholder 3:

▼ Major Expectations:

▼ Stakeholder 4:

▼ Major Expectations:

▼ Stakeholder 5:

▼ Major Expectations:

▼ Stakeholder 6:

▼ Major Expectations:

▼ Self
▼ Major Expectations:

Analyzing Ambiguity, Overload, and Conflict

After you identify key stakeholders' expectations, you might notice that three issues predominate: role ambiguity, role overload, and role conflict. The following provides some guidelines for dealing with each situation.

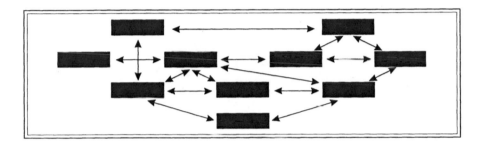

Role Ambiguity

One of the first things you will notice with respect to some stakeholders is that it is difficult to figure out what their expectations of you actually are or will be in the future. This is called *role ambiguity*. It is an increasingly important issue in organizations.

If you are experiencing such role ambiguity with respect to selected stakeholders, you have two choices.

1. Develop a communication process to reduce the ambiguity. Approach the stakeholders and ask them to share their expectations of you or provide your perceptions and ask for corrections.

---

2. Decide to "live with the ambiguity." Watch the stakeholders' future behavior for clues until you decipher what they want.

Obviously, the first alternative is the best *if* you can obtain "role clarification." You will have to take the initiative because the stakeholder probably is not aware that his or her expectations are unclear.

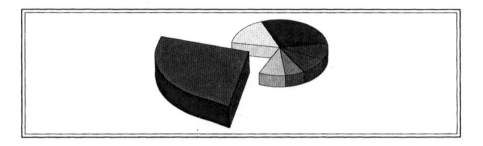

Role Overload

A second issue is *role overload*. This occurs when you realize that the sum of what your critical stakeholders expect of you far exceeds what you are able to do. If the stakeholders are not equally important, role overload typically is handled by ignoring the expectations of the less important stakeholders. However, this manner of coping often creates difficulties, because the ignored stakeholders may respond negatively.

A second coping mechanism for role overload is to compromise on each of the stakeholders' expectations by doing only a part of what each of them expects. Unfortunately, this may make you look relatively less competent in each of their eyes.

The best way of coping with role overload is to communicate the condition and to ask your key stakeholders to help you set priorities. You need to find out what is most important to them. These stakeholders may not even be aware of one another's expectations of you. Once you have communicated to them that you are overloaded, they can decide among themselves what is most important or they can choose to empower you to make the decision.

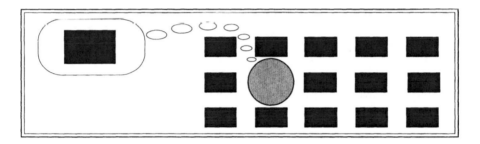

Role Conflict

Role conflict occurs when you realize that two or more stakeholders have conflicting expectations. This occurs most often in three forms.

1. What your superiors want conflicts with what your subordinates want

2. What one of your peer stakeholders wants conflicts with the expectations of another peer

3. What one of your critical stakeholders wants conflicts with your personal expectations

Each of us is a stakeholder in his or her own job, and we have personal expectations. Often, we are unwilling for any number of reasons to do what is expected of us. This leads to ethical, moral, and motivational dilemmas.

In each of these instances, role renegotiation with the stakeholders is essential so that the emotional cost of conflict can be minimized. This means that you must find a way to communicate to the various stakeholders how their expectations create conflict so that they can become involved in the resolution or decide to empower you to resolve the conflict. If you act unilaterally to resolve the conflict, you run the risk of disappointing a stakeholder and giving the impression that you are either not motivated or not competent to meet his or her expectations.

A special case of role overload or role conflict occurs when the expectations of family or friends conflict with the expectations of work stakeholders. This type of "work/family" overload and/or conflict is becoming more prevalent and will become an even larger problem as organizational boundaries loosen. For example, overload might be reduced if more work is done at home, but working at home may involve assumptions about responsibility and commitment that are out of line with current attitudes about organization/employee relationships. The solution to this kind of problem requires not only an understanding of the future form of organizations but also complex negotiations with both the work organization and the family and, ultimately, some change in cultural assumptions about the nature of work.

When you have finished analyzing your current job and roles, go on to the next step: Identifying changes in the environment.

CHAPTER 4

Step 2:
Identify Changes in the
Environment

Before completing this section, you may wish to
read Chapter 9, which discusses some of the
changes that are likely to occur in the future and
summarizes the major trends as they apply to jobs
and roles in organizations. Feel free to use this
material or any other pertinent material to help you
to project how the environment will change. Look
at changes five to ten years in the future, but don't
ignore trends that may have a more immediate
impact.

Four Dimensions of the Environment

It is useful to think of "the environment" in terms
of four different dimensions and to analyze possible changes in each of these dimensions. The dimensions are

1. **Technological** (e.g., the rapid evolution of information technology, biotechnology, etc.)

2. **Economic** (e.g., the globalization of markets and manufacturing processes, the growth of large trading blocks, increased global competition, etc.)

3. **Political** (e.g., the breakup of the Soviet Union, the fractionalization of countries such as Yugoslavia and Czechoslovakia into smaller ethnic units, etc.)

4. **Sociocultural** (e.g., the growing desire for democracy, the growth of human rights movements, environmentalism, etc.)

It is recommended that this analysis be done in a group, because other people's perceptions will trigger thoughts, leading to a deeper analysis. You may wish to brainstorm changes first and then sort the changes into the four categories later. Keep in mind that your ultimate goal in doing this analysis is to improve your understanding of how your stakeholders' expectations will change.

▼▼▼ *Future Environmental Trends*

 ▼ Technological Trends:

 ▼ Economic Trends:

 ▼ Political Trends:

 ▼ Sociocultural Trends:

▼ Other Relevant Trends:

CHAPTER 5

Step 3:
Assess Environmental Impacts on Stakeholder Expectations

▼▼▼ *Changes in Stakeholder Expectations*

Think of how the environmental trends you identified in Step 2 will affect each of the major stakeholders you identified in Step 1. and, in turn, how they
will change stakeholders' expectations of you.

▼ Stakeholder 1:

▼ Stakeholder 2:

▼ Stakeholder 3:

▼ Stakeholder 4:

▼ Stakeholder 5:

▼ Stakeholder 6:

▼ Self:

▼ Other Stakeholders Whose Expectations Will
Become Critical in the Future:

CHAPTER 6

Step 4:
Determine the Impact on
Job and Roles

▼▼▼ *Overall Impact on My Job and Roles*

Go back and revise your original job analysis from Step 1 in the light of your assessment of stakeholder changes. List below the primary impacts you perceive.

▼▼▼ *Impact on Job and Role Dimensions*

In the following list, review your job and role dimensions and rate each as you perceive it will change. Do this without looking at your previous ratings so that you can compare, with minimum bias, your perception of the job now and in the future.

Rate each dimension using the five-point scale: "1" is low; "5" is high.

	Low				High

1. Work with and in groups of various sorts (committees, task forces, meetings, etc.)   1 2 3 4 5

2. Operate as a consultant/catalyst in my day-to-day roles   1 2 3 4 5

3. Integrate the efforts of others who are technically more competent in their specialties than I am   1 2 3 4 5

4. Rely on secondhand information that is gathered by others   1 2 3 4 5

5. Monitor the thinking and decision making of others rather than doing it myself   1 2 3 4 5

	Low High
6. Facilitate the processes of management and decision making rather than making the decisions myself	1 2 3 4 5
7. Identify relevant problems and make sure that the right problems are worked on	1 2 3 4 5
8. Depend on others (peers, subordinates, etc.) for total performance (rather than it being within my own control)	1 2 3 4 5
9. Level of responsibility (accountability) is greater than my direct degree of control	1 2 3 4 5
10. Spend time considering the long-range health of the organization rather than its day-to-day performance	1 2 3 4 5

▼▼▼ *Job and Role Profile (Revised)*

Redo your job description in the light of the open-systems planning that you have done.

▼ Basic Responsibilities (Revised):

▼ Primary Resources for Getting the Job Done (Revised):

▼ Skills, Talents, and Attitudes Required to Do the Job (Revised):

CHAPTER 7

Step 5:
Redefine Job Requirements

What are the special skills, attitudes, and values that you will need to fulfill the job and roles as you now redefined them? To stimulate your thinking in this area, fill out the job characteristics profile below. Add any other dimensions that occur to you.

The items reflect the four categories that have been found to be relevant to effective organizational performance. Items that are particularly relevant to the rapidly changing environment in which future jobs and roles will exist have been emphasized.

▼▼▼ *Job Characteristics Profile*

For each of the items, put an X through the number that represents your perception of yourself in the *present* and put a circle around the number that represents what you think you *ought to be* in the future. Rate yourself using the five-point scale: "1" is low; "5" is high. If you are *not* a manager, fill out any items that pertain to your job and ignore the others.

▼ Motives and Values

	Low				High
1. Desire to get a job done, need for accomplishment	1	2	3	4	5
2. Commitment to my organization and its mission	1	2	3	4	5
3. Career aspirations and ambitions	1	2	3	4	5
4. Degree of involvement with career	1	2	3	4	5
5. Desire for high levels of responsibility	1	2	3	4	5
6. Desire to take risks	1	2	3	4	5
7. Desire to make tough decisions	1	2	3	4	5
8. Desire to work with and through people	1	2	3	4	5
9. Desire to exercise power and authority	1	2	3	4	5

	Low High
10. Desire to monitor and supervise the activities of others	1 2 3 4 5
11. Desire to delegate and help others to succeed	1 2 3 4 5
12. Desire to function as a general manager, free of functional and technical concerns	1 2 3 4 5
13. Desire to work collaboratively rather than competitively with others	1 2 3 4 5
14. Desire to learn	1 2 3 4 5
15. Desire to take risks even if that leads to errors	1 2 3 4 5

▼ Analytical Abilities and Skills

16. Ability to identify problems in complex, ambiguous situations	1 2 3 4 5
17. Ability to sense quickly what information is needed in relation to a complex problem	1 2 3 4 5
18. Ability to obtain needed information from others	1 2 3 4 5
19. Ability to assess the validity of information that I have not gathered myself	1 2 3 4 5

	Low				High
20. Ability to learn quickly from experience	1	2	3	4	5
21. Ability to detect errors in my own actions	1	2	3	4	5
22. Flexibility, my ability to think of and implement different solutions for different kinds of problems	1	2	3	4	5
23. Creativity, my ingenuity	1	2	3	4	5
24. Breadth of perspective—insight into a wide variety of situations	1	2	3	4	5
25. Degree of insight into myself (my strengths and weaknesses)	1	2	3	4	5

▼ Interpersonal and Group Skills

	Low				High
26. Ability to develop open and trusting relationships with peers	1	2	3	4	5
27. Ability to develop open and trusting relationships with superiors	1	2	3	4	5
28. Ability to develop open and trusting relationships with subordinates	1	2	3	4	5
29. Ability to listen to others in an understanding way	1	2	3	4	5

	Low	High
30. Ability to communicate my thoughts and ideas clearly and persuasively		1 2 3 4 5
31. Ability to communicate my feelings clearly		1 2 3 4 5
32. Ability to influence people over whom I have no direct control		1 2 3 4 5
33. Ability to influence my peers		1 2 3 4 5
34. Ability to influence my superiors		1 2 3 4 5
35. Ability to influence my subordinates		1 2 3 4 5
36. Ability to diagnose complex interpersonal and group situations		1 2 3 4 5
37. Ability to develop processes that ensure high-quality decisions without having to make the decisions myself		1 2 3 4 5
38. Ability to develop a climate of collaboration and teamwork		1 2 3 4 5
39. Ability to design processes to facilitate intergroup and interfunctional coordination		1 2 3 4 5
40. Ability to create a climate of growth and development for my subordinates		1 2 3 4 5

▼ Emotional Abilities and Skills

	Low	High

41. Degree to which I am able to make up my own mind without relying on the opinions of others   1 2 3 4 5

42. Degree to which I am able to share power with others   1 2 3 4 5

43. Degree to which I am able to tolerate and acknowledge errors   1 2 3 4 5

44. Degree of tolerance for ambiguity and uncertainty   1 2 3 4 5

45. Ability to take risks, to pursue a course of action even if it may produce negative consequences   1 2 3 4 5

46. Ability to pursue a course of action even if it makes me anxious and uncomfortable   1 2 3 4 5

47. Ability to confront and work through conflict situations (versus avoiding or suppressing them)   1 2 3 4 5

48. Ability to keep going after an experience of failure   1 2 3 4 5

	Low High
49. Ability to confront my stakeholders if there is role ambiguity, role overload, or role conflict	1 2 3 4 5
50. Ability to function in the face of continued environmental turbulence	1 2 3 4 5

▼ Other Items That Occur to You:

▼▼▼ *The Developmental Implications*

First look at those items where there is the greatest discrepancy between your present rating and where you think you should be. For each area where there is a significant discrepancy, create a developmental plan for yourself or figure out how to restructure the job so that your present capacity will be sufficient to do the job.

If you conclude that you must restructure your job, think that through in terms of renegotiating with the requisite stakeholders to ensure that the new expectations are realistic both from your point of view and from theirs.

List below the various developmental or restructuring actions you plan to take and keep this list as a point of reference to be reviewed at various times.

▼ Item No. _____
Developmental Plan:

▼ Item No. _____
Developmental Plan:

▼ Item No. _____
Developmental Plan:

▼ Item No. _____
Developmental Plan:

▼ Item No. _____
Developmental Plan:

▼ Item No. _____
Developmental Plan:

▼ Item No. _____
Developmental Plan:

▼ Item No. _____
Developmental Plan:

▼ Item No. _____
Developmental Plan:

▼ Item No. _____
Developmental Plan:

▼ Item No. _____
Developmental Plan:

▼ Item No. _____
Developmental Plan:

▼ Item No. _____
Developmental Plan:

▼ Item No. _____
Developmental Plan:

▼▼▼ *Developmental Summary*

Given the plans you have just made, what are the
next steps that you will take? Be specific and give a
timetable for each step.

▼ Step 1:

▼ Timetable:

▼ Step 2:

▼ Timetable:

▼ Step 3:

▼ Timetable:

Step 6:
Extend the Strategic Job
and Role Planning Activity

The final step in the activity is to think of
who else could benefit from the job-and-role-
planning activity and to expose those persons to
the idea and the process. They could be subordinates, peers, or superiors. Most likely, you will have
discovered in your stakeholder analysis that some
of them have unrealistic expectations and could
benefit from this kind of activity. This chapter will
examine reasons that support the need for job and
role planning. Share this information with others.

▼ List the names of people who would benefit from
job and role planning.

Why Job and Role Planning Is Critical to the Future

Job and role analysis and planning are increasingly important activities because work and organizations are changing at an ever more rapid rate, and all the indications are that work will become more fluid and will involve more complex relationships with others in superior, peer, and subordinate roles. The following are what I believe are some of the most important trends and their consequences for the nature of work. These trends all interact in complex ways and must be treated as a single system of forces, even though they are described one at a time.

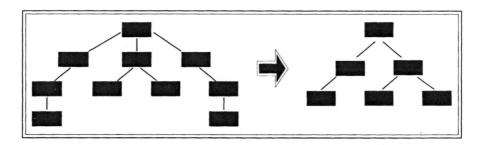

Organizations Are Restructuring Through "Downsizing" or "Rightsizing"

The Effects of Increased Competition

In order to remain competitive in an increasingly global marketplace, organizations are discovering the need to be concerned about perpetual improvement and stringent control of costs. This has led to a wave of layoffs and restructuring of organizations. As a result, many jobs have simply disappeared, and work has been reallocated and redesigned so that a smaller number of people can perform it.

The Formation of New Work Relationships

The possibilities inherent in the creative use of information technology, especially "groupware," have opened up new ways of thinking about work and jobs.[1] The way in which people will be connected to one another will vary and will require all kinds of new relationships. Strategic job and role planning will be a primary tool for assessing and reassessing those relationships. ·

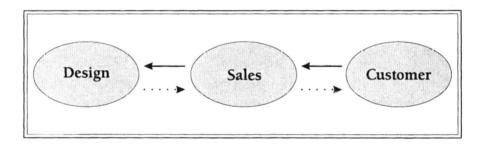

Globalization, New Technology, and "Right-sizing" Have Loosened the Boundaries of Organizations, Jobs, and Roles

At the organizational level, we see many industries loosening the boundaries between suppliers, manufacturers, and customers.[2] Using sophisticated information-technology tools, customers can directly access a company's sales organization, specify in detail what kinds of products or services they require, and get immediate prices and delivery dates from the computer.[3] As such systems become more common, the roles of purchasing agent and salesperson become much more ambiguous, and a chain reaction occurs throughout the organization that necessitates the redefinition of order processing, marketing, and even design and manufacturing.

The Effects of Automation on Job Roles

At the same time, the automation of everything from secretarial work to complex production processes makes all kinds of jobs much less manual and more conceptual.[4] Operators who work in automated refineries, nuclear power plants, paper mills, and other such organizations know as much about the running of their plants as the managers do. This creates new power relationships. The role of management becomes more ambiguous as managers no longer have the power of knowing things that their subordinates do not know. It is especially important for managers to discover that their relationships to their production workers fundamentally have changed and that workers have come to occupy a much more central position in the role network.

Operations

Support

As Work Becomes More Technically Complex, More People Will Work in Service and Staff Roles

The goal of automation generally is to reduce head count, but the more typical result is a redistribution of workers. Fewer operators are needed, but more support services are needed. The total cost of the operation ultimately may not change much, but the kinds of work that are performed will change radically. The relationships between sets of workers will, therefore, change in unknown ways. Operators have greater immediate responsibility for doing things right, but the programmers, systems engineers, and maintenance engineers have greater ultimate responsibility to keep the systems running—to keep the computers from "going down." Management becomes more of a coordinating and liaison function and less of a monitoring and control function. Peers in service roles come to be seen as much more central in the role network than they have been previously.

As Conceptual Work Increases and Job and Role Boundaries Loosen, Anxiety Levels Will Increase

Human organisms depend on certain levels of predictability and stability in their environments. Although we all have needs for creativity and stimulation, we may forget that those needs operate against a background of security, stability, and predictability.[5]

As organizations face increasing competitive pressures, as jobs become more conceptual, and as levels of responsibility in all jobs increase, we will see levels of stress and anxiety increase at all levels of the organization.[6] Formalization and bureaucracy has been one kind of defense against such anxiety, but the kind of work that needs to be done in the information and knowledge age requires more flexibility and innovation, thus making more anxiety an inevitable result.

Managing Anxiety

An increasing role for management will be the containment and working through of anxiety levels, although it is not at all clear by what individual or group mechanisms this will occur. When people are anxious, they want to be with others, so one of the most important functions of groups in organizations is the management of shared anxiety. The increasing emphasis on groups and teams may be the result not only of the growing complexity of work but also of the growing anxiety levels attending work.

The concept of sociotechnical systems has been promulgated for several decades, but as we project ahead, it would appear that it becomes a more important concept than ever.[7] One cannot separate the technical elements of a job from the social and political elements, as the network analysis in Step 1 is intended to illustrate. It also should be noted that job and role analysis and planning, when carried out regularly in a group setting, can be an anxiety reducer in that employees and managers can share their concerns about the loosening of boundaries and role overloads and conflicts while, at the same time, beginning to resolve them.

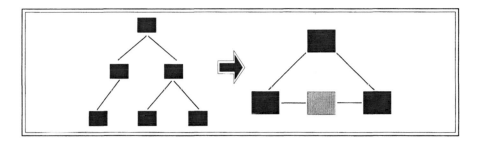

Organizations Are Flattening Hierarchical Structure and Empowering Employees

In the process of "rightsizing," organizations are

1. Reexamining their hierarchical structures

2. Moving toward flatter structures

3. Relying more on coordination mechanisms other than hierarchy

4. "Empowering" their employees in various ways

Work Organization by Project

In the flat, project-based organization of the future, power and authority will rotate among different project leaders, and individual project members will have to coordinate their own activities across a number of projects with different leaders. Operational authority will shift rapidly from one project leader to another, and individual employees may find themselves working for several bosses simultaneously. At the same time, as knowledge and information are more widely distributed, employees will become empowered *de facto* because, increasingly, they will know things that their bosses do not know.

The Role of Hierarchy

Hierarchy is fairly intrinsic to human systems, so we will probably not see the abandonment of hierarchical structures so much as a change in their function.[8] For example, broad hierarchical categories such as civil-service grades, degrees of partnership in a law firm, or levels of professorial rank may continue to serve broad career-advancement functions but may not be good guides as to who will have operational authority over a task or project.

Respect for people and the amount of influence they exert will have more to do with their operational performance than with their formal rank, and hierarchy increasingly will be viewed as a necessary adjunct to organizational life rather than its prime principle.

Authority and Compensation

Power and authority will derive from what a person knows and what skills he or she has demonstrated. Because conceptual knowledge is largely invisible, the opportunities will increase for misperception or conflicting perceptions of who knows what and who should be respected for what. This will make the exercise of authority and influence much more problematic, which, in turn, will increase anxiety levels in organizations. By bringing groups together to do job and role analysis and planning, one can help to contain this anxiety and, more importantly, overcome the limitations of traditional job analysis, which attempts to evaluate the level of each job. One can speculate, in this regard, that pay will be tied more to formal rank, length of service, and number of skills that an employee has, not the particular job he or she is doing at any given moment.

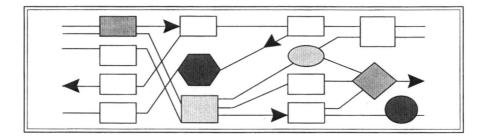

Organizations Are Becoming More Differentiated and Complex

With the rapid growth of technology in all fields of endeavor, the number of products and services available is increasing. At the same time, growing affluence and more widely distributed information about products and services are creating more demanding consumers. Therefore organizations are having to respond by developing their ability to deliver products and services faster, in greater variety, to more places all over the globe.[9]

The Integration of Increasingly Differentiated Specialists

One of the major consequences is that the organizations that make the products and/or deliver the services have to be more differentiated and complex. That, in turn, means that there will be more and different kinds of occupational specialists to be managed, and whose efforts must somehow be tied together into a coherent organizational whole.

Many of these specialists are neither motivated nor able to talk to one another, which creates special problems of integration of effort.[10] The highly specialized design engineer working in the research and development end of the company often has little in common with the financial analyst whose specialty is the management of the company's investment portfolio or the personnel specialist who is concerned with the most recent affirmative-action legislation. Yet all of these and many other specialists contribute in major ways to the welfare of the total organization, and their efforts have to be integrated. Such integration cannot take place unless all the specialists and managers involved become conscious of one another as stakeholders and begin to make an effort to respond to one another's expectations.

The Effects of Specialization on Career Development

Beyond this, senior management must begin to worry about and plan for the specific career development of such specialists, because many of them will be neither able nor willing to go into managerial positions.[11] Such developmental planning cannot occur without a clear understanding of the role networks within which these specialists operate and the involvement of those employees in planning their own development.

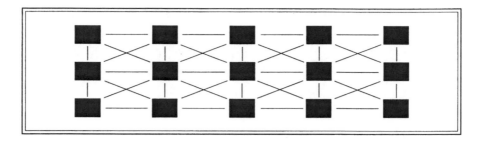

Organizational Subunits Are Becoming More Interdependent

The Growing Need for Coordination and Integration

In order to produce a complex product or service effectively over a period of time, the many subspecialties of the organization will have to be coordinated and integrated because they are simultaneously and sequentially interdependent in a variety of ways. For example, if the financial department does not manage the company's cash supply adequately, there is less opportunity for capital expansion or R & D; on the other hand, if an engineering design sacrifices some elements of quality for low cost, the result may be customer complaints, a lowered company reputation, and the subsequent decreased ability of the company to borrow money for capital expansion. In this sense, engineering and finance are highly interdependent, even though each may be highly specialized and neither may interact with the other directly.

Sequential interdependence is the more common situation. The engineering department cannot design a product or service if R & D has not done a good job of developing the concept or prototype; in turn, manufacturing cannot build the product if engineering has produced unbuildable designs; and sales and marketing cannot do their jobs well if they have poor products to sell. Of course, R & D cannot get its concepts right if marketing has not given it clear descriptions of future customer needs, and the process innovations that occur within manufacturing often influence both marketing and engineering in terms of the types of products that are thought to be conceivable and feasible.

These types of interdependence always have existed within organizations, but as specialization increases, interdependence also increases because the final product or service is more complex and more vulnerable to any of its elements malfunctioning. Nowhere is this clearer than in computer products and services. The hardware and software have to be designed properly in the first place and then implemented by a variety of specialists who serve as the interfaces between the final users and the computer system. If any one of the specialists fails to do his or her job, the entire service or product may fail.

Revealing Interdependent Relationships

Job and role analysis and planning is designed to expose these interdependencies through analysis of the role network and the identification of key stakeholders. What often is most surprising as one does the analysis is the large number of stakeholders whom one must take into account simultaneously.

And, as one looks ahead, that number is growing, so the skills involved in dealing with multiple stakeholder expectations become more and more central to organizational performance.[12]

Organizational Climates Are Becoming More Collaborative and Cooperative

One major effect of the recognition of increased interdependence is that competition between organizational units or individuals is perceived as potentially destructive. Teamwork and collaborative/cooperative relations are increasingly thought of as necessary to get the job done. This trend runs counter to the external marketplace philosophy that competition is a good thing, but it increasingly is seen to be a necessary adaptation within organizations, even if *inter*organizational relations continue to be competitive.

Interorganizational Collaboration

If this trend is worldwide, we will begin to see more evidence of interorganizational collaboration as well, not for political reasons but for practical reasons of technological necessity. Increased levels of coordination will not be achieved by more centralized planning, as was attempted in the communist/socialist economies, but by more distribution of information and decentralization, which will permit the various units to coordinate among themselves. However, for this self-managed coordination to occur, not only must information be widely available, but all of the actors in the system must be able to decipher their roles in it. The same information can be framed and interpreted in many different ways. For collaboration and cooperation to work, common frames of reference must be established, and that process will involve organizational members in much more group and team activity. Building shared frames of reference also increasingly will become a primary task of leadership.[13]

The Transition From a Competitive to a Collaborative Environment

This trend poses a particular dilemma for managers whose own careers have developed in very competitive environments and who simply do not have the interpersonal competence to redesign their organizational processes to be more supportive of collaborative relations. I have met many a manager who pays lip service to "teamwork" but whose day-to-day style sends clear signals of not really understanding or supporting the concept, with the predictable consequence that this person's "team" does not function as a team at all. Unfortunately, both the manager and the subordinates may draw the erroneous conclusion that it is the teamwork *concept* that is at fault rather than their failure to *implement* the concept. Once they understand the nature of the network they are in, they can do a better job of implementation. Thus, the very activity of job and role planning, when carried out by a team, becomes an important team-building function.

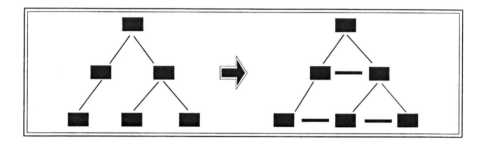

Organizations Are Becoming More Dependent on Lateral Communication Channels

Closely connected with the need for more collaborative work is the need for information to flow laterally between technical specialists rather than going through a hierarchy. For example, some companies are putting the product-development and marketing departments closer to each other geographically and stimulating direct contact between them rather than having higher levels of management attempt to translate marketing issues for the development people. The customer, the salesperson, and the marketing specialist in a complex industry such as electronics all probably know more about the technical side of the business than the general manager does and, therefore, must be brought into direct interaction with the designer and engineer if a usable product or service is to result.

Jay Galbraith[14] has argued very convincingly that the information-processing needs of organizations based on task complexity and environmental uncertainty are, in fact, the major determinants of organizational structure and that hierarchical structures work only so long as task complexity and uncertainty are fairly low. Lateral structures such as project teams, task forces, ad hoc committees, cross-functional organizational units, and matrix management become more common with increased complexity and uncertainty.

The Transition to Lateral Communication

It is technological possibilities and consumer demands that are driving business toward greater complexity, and it will be information technology that will make it possible for organizations eventually to adapt by creating the kinds of lateral communication that will make coordination, integration, and genuine teamwork possible.

Here again, managers face a novel situation because of the likelihood that their own careers have been spent in organizational settings dedicated to principles of hierarchy and chains of command. In such "traditional" organizations, communication with people outside the chain of command is discouraged and punished. Not only will the organizational reward system and climate have to shift to encourage lateral communication but, in addition, managers will have to be trained to create lateral structures and to make them work. Job and role planning will facilitate this trend by showing how many of the key stakeholders are neither superiors nor subordinates but various peer relationships in which interdependence exists.

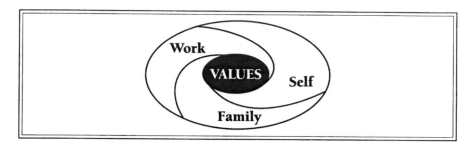

Sociocultural Values Concerning Family, Self, and Work Are Changing

In this section, I will refer mostly to trends that have been observed in the United States.

Traditional Concepts of Loyalty and Authority Are Being Supplanted by an Emphasis on Individuality

People are placing less value on traditional concepts of organizational loyalty and the acceptance of authority based on formal position, age, or seniority, and are placing more value on individualism and individual rights vis-a-vis the organization. Increasingly, people are demanding

- That the tasks they are asked to perform make sense and provide them with some challenge and opportunity to express their talents.
- That the rights of individuals be protected, especially if the individuals are members of minority groups or are likely to be discriminated against on some arbitrary basis such as sex, age, disability, religion, or ethnic origin.
- Some voice in decisions that affect them.

This is leading to the growth of various forms of industrial democracy, participative management, and worker involvement in job design and corporate decision making. As was noted earlier, from the point of view of the employing organization, worker involvement makes sense to the extent that the trend toward specialization of tasks is occurring. For many kinds of decisions, it is the worker who has the key information and who, therefore, must be involved if the decision is to be a sound one. Thus, employee "empowerment" has taken on almost fad status.

People Are Devaluing Work As a "Success" Yardstick

People are placing less value on work or career as a total life concern and less value on promotion or hierarchical movement within the organization as the sole measure of "success."

- More value is being placed on leading a balanced life in which work, career, family, and self-development all receive their fair share of attention.

— "Success" increasingly is defined in terms of the full use of all of one's talents and in contributing not only to one's work organization but also to one's family, community, and self.

Careers are built on different career anchors. The measure of success and advancement varies with whether one is oriented around the managerial, technical/functional, security, autonomy, entrepreneurial, service, pure challenge, or lifestyle anchor.[15]

People Are Redefining Sexual Roles

People are placing less value on traditional concepts of male and female sex roles with respect to both work and family. In the career and work areas, we are seeing a growing trend toward equal employment opportunities for men and women, a breakdown of sex-role stereotypes in regard to work (e.g., more women are going into engineering and more men are going into nursing), and a similar breakdown of sex-role stereotypes in regard to family roles (e.g., more women are becoming the primary "breadwinners," and more men are staying home to take care of children, do the cooking, and clean the house). Our society is opening up the range of choices for both men and women to pursue new kinds of work, family roles, and lifestyles.[16] Two of the major changes are the "dual-career" family, in which both husband and wife are committed to career development, and the single-parent family. These changes are forcing organizations to develop new personnel policies and are forcing social institutions to develop new options for childcare.

One of the most important elements of job and role planning is to determine the positions of spouses or significant others, children, and friends in the role network and as key stakeholders. As dual career families and single parents become more common, one will see complex, overlapping role networks in households, requiring more complex, adaptive solutions both at work and at home.[17]

Economic Growth Is Weighed Against Environmental Concerns

People are placing less value on economic growth and are placing relatively more value on conserving and protecting the quality of the environment in which they live. Assessing the impact of technology is becoming a major activity in our society. We see increased willingness to stop progress even in economically depressed areas if the environment would be endangered (e.g., reluctance to build the supersonic transport or to allow our airports to admit existing SSTs; highway construction that comes to an abrupt halt in the middle of a city; and refusal to build new oil refineries). However, as we saw in the early 1990s, during recessionary periods, economic growth values resurface, and conflict increases between the need to protect the environment and the need for jobs.

These value changes and conflicts have created a situation in which the incentives and rewards offered by the different parts of our society have become much more diverse and, consequently, much less integrated. We see this most clearly in the organizational generation gap—older managers or employees who are still operating from a "Protestant work ethic" versus young employees who question arbitrary authority, meaningless work, organizational loyalty, restrictive personnel policies, and fundamental corporate goals and prerogatives. As options and choices have opened up and managers have begun to question the traditional success ethic, they are more

— Ready to refuse promotions or relocations
— Willing to "retire on the job" while pursuing family activities or off-the-job hobbies
— Likely to resign from high-potential careers to pursue "second careers" that are perceived to be more challenging and/or rewarding by criteria other than formal hierarchical position or salary.

What all this means for the managers of tomorrow is that they will have to manage in a much more "pluralistic" society, one in which employees at all levels will have more choices and will exercise those choices. Managers will not only have to exhibit more personal flexibility in dealing with the range and variety of individual needs they encounter in subordinates, peers, and superiors, but will also have to learn how to influence organizational policies with respect to

— Recruitment
— Work assignment

- Pay and benefit systems
- Working hours and length of work week
- Attitudes about dual employment of couples
- Support of educational activities at a much higher scale
- Development of childcare facilities, etc.

With respect to all these issues, the manager will be caught in the middle among several key stakeholders. These include

- Government agencies, with respect to discrimination (on the basis of sex, age, race, and other characteristics), environmental issues, and occupational safety issues
- Community-interest groups, with respect to equal rights, protection of the environment, product quality and safety, and other forms of consumerism
- Stockholders who are eager to maintain an efficient and profitable operation and a fair return on their investments
- Customers, with respect to growing needs for variety, rapid delivery, higher quality, and better service
- Competitors

— Employees—whether unionized or not—who are anxious to improve the quality of working life, create flexible corporate policies, provide challenging and meaningful work, and be responsible "corporate citizens"
— Family and self in terms of a need to maintain a balanced life

Role ambiguity, role overload, and role conflict are likely to be chronic conditions, and the processes of setting priorities and negotiating with different stakeholders are likely to be perpetual rather than one-time activities. Boundaries of all kinds will be perpetually defined and redefined, and anxiety levels around those activities periodically will be very high. We see this at the international level in the tension resulting from globalization on the one hand, and the breaking up of countries into ethnic or cultural units on the other hand, even if those units will have a difficult time surviving economically as nations.

The Future

The trends identified previously are themselves not stable. In fact, if there is anything to be learned from the last few decades, it is that our ability to predict is declining rapidly. The management of "surprise" is the order of the day. For example, we cannot really predict the future economic impact of the Asian bloc of countries (especially China) or the future behavior of the European Economic Community. We cannot predict the rate at which the formerly socialist or communist countries will become politically or economically viable and, when they do, what impact that will have on the global scene.

We cannot predict the rate at which information and biotechnology will evolve low-cost products and services that will fundamentally change the nature of work, the nature of organizations, and the nature of life itself. The potential ethical issues implicit in bioengineering boggle the mind.

On the political front, we cannot predict the outcome of the simultaneous trends toward globalization and fractionation into smaller, ethnically pure countries. As of this writing, the role of the United States and of the United Nations remains unclear and unpredictable in the conflict between Serbians and Bosnians or between Israelis and Palestinians and in aid to starving nations. We cannot predict the outcome of the confrontation between North Korea an the rest of the world over their nuclear proliferation, nor the effect of incipient civil wars all over Africa.

Within the U.S., we cannot predict what will happen to the budget deficit, how health-care costs will be brought under control while health-care delivery is improved, how our educational system will be revitalized, and how we will solve the racial problems in our inner cities. Our current systems of governance are strained and possibly not up to the tasks facing us.

What all of this means is that we must become *perpetual learners*. As a growing number of observers and analysts have noted, it will be the ability to learn that will make the difference in the future.[18] If we cannot cope with surprise and develop new ways of framing problems and new responses, we will become less effective. Ultimately, this puts more emphasis on dynamic processes, on learning to live with perpetual change, and on developing the diagnostic skills that permit us to see what is needed.

It is this need for dynamic processes that leads us back to job and role analysis and planning. Projecting this to the extreme suggests that job and role planning should become virtually a perpetual activity that is integral to the management process itself. Every time there is a new project or a new assignment, the manager and his or her subordinate should do a brief version of job and role planning to ensure that there is consensus on what will need to be done and who will need to be involved. Job descriptions will become dynamic documents, perpetually renegotiated as the work of the organization changes in response to changing environmental circumstances.

Perpetual job and role planning will require much higher levels of interaction among members of the organization, especially between managers and their subordinates. On the one hand, such an increase in meetings will increase frustration because of the time it will take, but, paradoxically, people will discover that such meetings are the best way of coping with the increasing anxiety that future jobs and roles will precipitate. Job and role planning will provide opportunities for supportive role negotiation that will reduce anxiety while, at the same time, increasing our conceptual understanding of what we must do to best fulfill our own needs and those of the organization.

CHAPTER 9

Conclusions and Implications

Successful organizational performance and productive, satisfying careers ultimately are the results of a good process of matching the ever-changing needs of organizations with the ever-changing needs of individual career occupants. As the rate of change increases, the matching challenge will be greater than ever.

The individual career occupant has a responsibility to know what he or she wants and requires from his or her career and job. Such insight comes from experience and from systematic self-diagnosis. We all should know what our career anchors are so that we can make better choices and negotiate better with organizations when we are confronted with job opportunities and options. But what of the organization's responsibility?

I believe that organizations have not done well in understanding the work to be done to meet organizational needs, and even when they do understand the work to be done, they have not done a good job of communicating their needs and expectations.

The primary purpose of strategic job and role planning is to improve the process of planning and diagnosing work and of communicating the diagnosis to job incumbents. In other words, individuals cannot do their jobs well and make good career choices if the information about the work and their career options is incomplete, superficial, or inaccurate.

The organization is an abstraction, but the individual employee is not. I am arguing that all employees (including managers), as part of their basic jobs, must have a complete understanding of their own work and the work to be done under, around, and above them and must have the skill to communicate that understanding to the subordinates, peers, and superiors who must carry out the work. Inasmuch as the work is perpetually changing, the employee must perpetually think about and plan for all the activities that he or she is responsible for or connected with. The exercises presented in this book are designed to facilitate such planning and are, therefore, an integral tool in the process of fulfilling both individual and organizational needs.

Endnotes

Chapter 8

1. R. Johansen, et al., *Leading Business Teams* (Reading, MA: Addison-Wesley, 1991).

2. T.A. Kochan and M. Useem, eds., *Transforming Organizations* (New York: Oxford University Press, 1992).

3. S.M. Davis and B. Davidson, *2020 Vision* (New York: Simon and Schuster, 1991).

4. S. Zuboff, *In the Age of the Smart Machine: The Future of Work* (New York: Basic Books, 1988).

5. E.H. Schein, *Organizational Culture and Leadership,* 2nd ed. (San Francisco, CA: Jossey-Bass, 1992).

6. L. Hirschhorn, *The Workplace Within* (Cambridge, MA: MIT Press, 1988).; S. Zuboff, *In the Age of the Smart Machine: The Future of Work* (New York: Basic Books, 1988).

7. L.D. Ketchum and E. Trist, *All Teams Are Not Created Equal* (Newbury Park, CA: Sage, 1992).

8. E.H. Schein, "Reassessing the 'Divine Rights' of Managers," *Sloan Management Review,* 30(3) (1989): 63-68.

9. S.M. Davis and B. Davidson, *2020 Vision* (New York: Simon and Schuster, 1991).

10. E.H. Schein, *Organizational Culture and Leadership,* 2nd ed. (San Francisco, CA: Jossey-Bass, 1992).

11. E.H. Schein, *Career Anchors: Discovering Your Real Values* (San Diego, CA: Pfeiffer and Company, 1993).

12. S.A. Rosell, ed., *Governing in an Information Society* (Montreal, Quebec: Institute for Research on Public Policy, 1992).

13. S.A. Rosell, ed., *Governing in an Information Society* (Montreal, Quebec: Institute for Research on Public Policy, 1992).; E.H. Schein, *Organizational Culture and Leadership,* 2nd ed. (San Francisco, CA: Jossey-Bass, 1992).

14. J. Galbraith, *Designing Complex Organizations* (Reading, MA: Addison-Wesley, 1973).

15. E.H. Schein, *Career Anchors: Discovering Your Real Values* (San Diego, CA: Pfeiffer and Company, 1993).

16. L. Bailyn, "Accommodation of Work to Family," in *Working Couples,* R. Rapoport and R.N. Rapoport (New York: Harper and Row, 1978).; L. Bailyn, "Changing the Conditions of Work: Implications for Career Development," in *Career Development in the 1990s: Theory and Practice,* ed. D.H. Montross and C.J. Schinkman (Springfield, IL: Thomas, 1992).

17. L. Baylin, *Breaking the Mold* (New York: Free Press, 1993)

18. D.N. Michael, "Governing by Learning in an Information Society," in *Governing in an Information Society,* ed. S.A. Rosell (Montreal, Quebec: Institute for Research on Public Policy, 1992).; S.A. Rosell, ed., *Governing in an Information Society* (Montreal, Quebec: Institute for Research on Public Policy, 1992).; T.J. Peters, *Thriving on Chaos* (New York: Knopf, 1987).; P.M. Senge, *The Fifth Discipline* (New York: Doubleday Currency, 1990).

Chapter 9

1. E.H. Schein, *Career Anchors: Discovering Your Real Values* (San Diego, CA: Pfeiffer and Company, 1993).

Bibliography

Allen, T.J. *Managing the Flow of Technology.* Cambridge, MA: MIT Press, 1977.

Bailyn, L. "Accommodation of Work to Family," in *Working Couples,* R. Rapoport and R.N. Rapoport. New York: Harper and Row, 1978.

——— . Breaking the Mold (New York: Free Press, 1993)

——— . "Changing the Conditions of Work: Implications for Career Development," in *Career Development in the 1990s: Theory and Practice,* ed. D.H. Montross and C.J. Schinkman. Springfield, IL: Thomas, 1992.

Davis, S.M. and B. Davidson. *2020 Vision.* New York: Simon and Schuster, 1991.

Davis, S.M. and P.R. Lawrence. *Matrix.* Reading, MA: Addison-Wesley, 1977.

Galbraith, J. *Designing Complex Organizations.* Reading, MA: Addison-Wesley, 1973.

Hirschhorn, L. *The Workplace Within.* Cambridge, MA: MIT Press, 1988.

Johansen, R., et al. *Leading Business Teams*. Reading, MA: Addison-Wesley, 1991.

Ketchum, L.D. and E. Trist. *All Teams Are Not Created Equal*. Newbury Park, CA: Sage, 1992.

Kochan, T.A. and M. Useem, eds. *Transforming Organizations*. New York: Oxford University Press, 1992.

Michael, D.N. "Governing by Learning in an Information Society," in *Governing in an Information Society,* ed. S.A. Rosell. Montreal, Quebec: Institute for Research on Public Policy, 1992.

Peters, T.J. *Thriving on Chaos*. New York: Knopf, 1987.

Rosell, S.A. ed. *Governing in an Information Society*. Montreal, Quebec: Institute for Research on Public Policy, 1992.

Savage, C.M. *Fifth Generation Management: Integrating Enterprises Through Human Networking*. Maynard, MA: Digital Press, 1990.

Schein, E.H. *Career Dynamics: Matching Individual and Organizational Needs*. Reading, MA: Addison-Wesley, 1978.

——— . "Reassessing the 'Divine Rights' of Managers," *Sloan . Management Review,* 30(3) 1989: 63-68.

——— . *Career Anchors: Discovering Your Real Values.* San Diego, CA: Pfeiffer and Company, 1993.

——— . *Organizational Culture and Leadership*, 2nd ed. San Francisco, CA: Jossey-Bass, 1992.

Scott-Morton, M.S. ed. *The Corporation of the 1990s*. New York: Oxford University Press, 1991.

Senge, P.M. *The Fifth Discipline*. New York: Doubleday Currency, 1990.

Zuboff, S. *In the Age of the Smart Machine: The Future of Work*. New York: Basic Books, 1988.

Index

A

Automation
    effect on job roles, 64
    goal of, 65
Autonomy, job, 3

B

Balance, emphasis on, 79
Biotechnology, evolution of, 85
Brainstorming, environmental change and, 37

C

Career development, specialization and, 71
Career Dynamics: Matching Individual and Organizational Needs, x
Career goals, evaluating, x
Careers, matching to organizational needs, 89
Chemical industry, job and role planning in, 6-7
Childcare, options for, 80
Choices, societal support for, 80-81
Collaborative/cooperative relations, in organizations, 74-76
Collaborative environment, transition to, 75-76
Communication. *See also* Information
    of expectations, 3
    in organizations, 76-78
    concerning role ambiguity, 29
    role overload and, 31
Community-interest groups, as key stakeholders, 83

Developmental plans,
   formulating, 56-59
Discrimination, protection against, 79
"Downsizing," implications
   of, 62-63
Dual-career families, 80-81
Dynamic job elements, xi
Dynamic processes, need for, 86

E

Economic dimension of environments, 36
Economic growth, changing views of, 81-84
Economic trends, brain-storming, 38
Emotional abilities, assessment of, 54-55
Employees
   empowerment of, 67-69, 79
   expectations of, 11
   job and role analysis by, 3
   job and role planning by, x-xi
   as key stakeholders, 84
   responsibilities of, 90
Engineering departments,
   interdependence of, 72-73
Environment
   concern about, 81-84
   dimensions of, 35-37

Environmental change. *See also* Work environment
  analyzing, 5
  identifying, 16, 35-39
  projections of, 4
Environmental impacts
  on jobs and roles, 17, 45-48
  on stakeholder expectations, 41-44
Environmental stability, need for, 66
Environmental trends, analyzing, 38-39
Equal employment opportunities, 80-81
Evaluation, of jobs, 21-22. *See also* Assessment
Executive positions, job and role analysis and planning for, 9
Expectations communication of, 3
  of employees, 11
  of line managers, 10-11
  of senior management, 10
  stakeholder, 26-28, 41-44
  unrealistic, 61
External interfaces, handling, 7
External marketplace philosophy, 74

F

Family changing views of, 78-81
  as a key stakeholder, 84
  in the role network, 81
Family roles, changes in, 80-81

G

Galbraith, Jay, 77
Globalization, 12, 36
   effects of, 63-64
   need for, 70
   outcome of, 85
   tension arising from, 84
Government, as a key stakeholder, 83
Grievance process, 11
Groups
   management of anxiety by, 66-67
   working with, 46
Group skills, assessment of, 52-53
"Groupware," 63

H

Hierarchical movement, devaluation of, 79
Hierarchical structure, changes in, 67-69
Hierarchy, role of, 68-69
HR managers, job and role analysis with, 10-11. *See also Management*
Human resource management,
   complexity of, 10-12
   professional community of, 11
Human resource planning, xi,
   versus job and role planning, 1, 2

I

Individualism, emphasis on, 78-79
Individual needs, fulfilling, 90
Individual rights, protection of, 79
Industrial democracy, 79
Information. *See also* Communication; Lateral communication
   about career options, 90
   availability of, 75
Information technology. *See also* Technology
   evolution of, 85
   lateral communication and, 77
   use of, 63
Integration, need for, 72-73
Integration of effort, problems with, 70-71
Integration skills, 46
Interdependent relationships, exposing, 73-74
Interorganizational collaboration, 74-75
Interpersonal skills, assessment of, 52-53

J

Job analysis
   job and role planning versus, 1
   revising, 45
Job and role analysis
   annual, 3
   for executive positions, 9
   power of, 8

disappearance of, 61

environmental impacts on, 17, 45-48

evaluating, x

fluid boundaries of, 2-3

future expectations about, 5

inventorying, 15-16, 19-33

organizational context of, 5

questions concerning, 2

reviewing, 13-14

role network surrounding, 1

spontaneous redesign of, 8-9

K

Key stakeholders. *See also* Stakeholders
   effect of changes on, 5
   identifying, 1, 4, 26-28, x
   types of, 10-11, 83-84
   understanding, xiii

L

Lateral communication, transition to, 77-78. *See also*
   Communication; Information

Lateral communication channels, 76-78

Leadership, role of, 75. *See also* Management

Learning, need for, 85-86

Line managers, expectations of, 10–11
Loyalty, changing views of, 78–79

M

Management changing nature of, 6–7
   changing values of, 82
   collaborative relations and, 75
   containment of anxiety by, 66–67
   creation of lateral structures by, 77–78
   facilitating, 47
   interaction with
   subordinates, 86
   liaison function of, 65
   role ambiguity in, 64
"Management of surprise," 84
Management system, redesign of, 9
Managers
   job and role analysis by, 3
   job and role planning by, x–xi
Manufacturing departments, interdependence of, 73
Marketing departments, interdependence of, 73
Matrix management, 77
Motives, assessment of, 50–51
Multicultural environments, working in, 12

N

Negotiation of job restructuring, 56
   as a role of management, 7 of roles, 32, 86–87
New work relationships, formation of, 63

O

Occupational specialists, management of, 70–71
Open-systems planning, 3
   applying to jobs and roles, 3–13
   elements of, 4–5
Operational authority decisions about, 69
   shifting of, 68
Organizational boundaries, loosening of, 63–64
Organizational climate, changes in, 74–76
Organizational generation gap, 82
Organizational health, assessing, 47
Organizational mission, fulfilling, 4
Organizational performance
   categories of, 49–55
   successful, 89
Organizational policy, influencing, 83
Organizational subunits, interdependence of, 72–74
Organizational trends, 62–87

future trends in, 85

Potential, appraising, 7

Power. *See also* Authority
   rotation of, 68
   skills-based, 69

Power relationships, changes in, 64

Priorities, role overload and, 31

Problems, defining, 47

Project-based work organization, 68

Project teams, 77

Public relations, importance of, 8-9

R

Resources, job, 20

"Retirement on the job," 82

Reward systems, 4
   changes in, 77

"Rightsizing"
   effects of, 63-64, 67-69
   implications of, 62-63

Role ambiguity
   analyzing, 29-30
   as a chronic condition, 84

Role boundaries, loosening of, 63-64, 66-67

Role clarification, obtaining, 29, 30

Role conflict, dealing with, 31-33

Role dimensions, rating, 46-48

Role negotiation, 86-87

Role network, 1
    identifying, 4, 23-25
    position of the family in, 81
    sample, 24
    service roles and, 65
    understanding, 71
    worker position in, 64
Role overload, 11
    handling, 30-31
Role planning. *See* Job and role planning
Roles
    applying open-systems planning to, 3-13
    environmental impacts on, 17, 45-48
    fluid boundaries of, 2-3
    future expectations about, 5
    inventorying, 15-16, 19-33
    spontaneous redesign of, 8-9
Role switching, ix

S

Sales departments, interdependence of, 73
"Second careers," 82
Self, changing views of, 78-81
Self-diagnosis, 89
Self-insight, importance of, 3
Senior management, expectations of, 10. *See also* Management
Sequential interdependence, 72-73
Service roles, increase in, 65

"Servicing the line" function, 11
Sexual roles, redefinition of, 80–81
Single-parent families, 80
Skills
    assessment of, 51–55
    job-related, 20
Society, pluralism of, 82
Sociocultural dimension of environments, 36
Sociocultural trends, brainstorming, 39
Sociotechnical systems, 67
"Soft" skills, training in, 7
Specialists
    communication among, 76
    occupational, 70–71
Specialization
    effects of, 71
    trend toward, 79
Specialties, coordination and integration of, 72–73
Stakeholder analysis, 6–7
Stakeholder expectations
    changes in, 41–44
    environmental impacts on, 16-17, 41–44
Stakeholder/role network, 15
Stakeholders. *See also* Key stakeholders
    accounting for, 73–74
    categories of, 23
    expectations of, 32
Stereotypes, sex-role, 80–81
Strategic job and role planning, ix-x. *See also* Job and role planning

Strategic options, understanding, 4
Stress, managing, 66-67
Subordinates, dependence on, 47
Success, measures of, 79
Success ethic, traditional, 82

T

Talents, use of, 79, 80
Task forces, 77
Teamwork
    emphasis on, 66-67
    implementation of, 75-76
    increase in, 74-76
Technological change, dealing with, 6
Technological dimension of environments, 36
Technological trends, brainstorming, 38
Technology. *See also* Automation; Information technology
    assessing the impact of, 81
    effects of, 63-64
    growth of, 70
    interorganizational collaboration and, 74-75
Traditional organizations, 77
Trends
    analyzing, 38-39
    future, 84-87
    organizational, 62-87

V

Values
    assessment of, 50-51
    changes in, 80-82

W

Work
    changing views of, 78-81
    increasing complexity of, 65
    as a "success" yardstick, 79-80
Work environment
    changes in, xiii, 1
    dynamic nature of, 9
Worker involvement, increase in, 79
Worker-management relations, 64
Workers, redistribution of, 65
Work/family overload, 32
Work organization, project-based, 68
Work relationships
    changes in, 63, 65
    complexity of, 62

Printed in the United States
66098LVS00003B/180

9 780893 842413